JESUS
LOVES
YOU

Contact Us:

MyBibleWorkbooks@gmail.com

Projectkingdomcome

Projectkingdomcome

PROJECT KINGDOM COME
ISBN: 978-1-961786-06-6

Get The Entire Workbook Series!

SCAN ME

THE BOOK OF
GENESIS
BIBLE-BASED WORKBOOK

Take an adventure into the amazing Book of Genesis and test your knowledge as you go!

PROJECT KINGDOM COME

THE BOOKS OF
EXODUS & JOSHUA
BIBLE-BASED WORKBOOK

Take an adventure into the amazing Books of Exodus and Joshua and test your knowledge as you go!

PROJECT KINGDOM COME

THE BOOKS OF
I & II SAMUEL
BIBLE-BASED WORKBOOK

Take an adventure into the amazing Books of 1st and 2nd Samuel and test your knowledge as you go!

PROJECT KINGDOM COME

THE BOOKS OF
I & II KINGS
BIBLE-BASED WORKBOOK

Take an adventure into the amazing Books of 1st and 2nd Kings and test your knowledge as you go!

PROJECT KINGDOM COME

THE BOOKS OF
ESTHER & RUTH
BIBLE-BASED WORKBOOK

Take an adventure into the amazing Books of Esther and Ruth and test your knowledge as you go!

PROJECT KINGDOM COME

THE BOOKS OF
DANIEL & JOB
BIBLE-BASED WORKBOOK

Take an adventure into the amazing Books of Daniel and Job and test your knowledge as you go!

PROJECT KINGDOM COME

THE BOOK OF
MATTHEW
BIBLE-BASED WORKBOOK

Take an adventure into the amazing Book of Matthew and test your knowledge as you go!

PROJECT KINGDOM COME

THE BOOK OF
MARK
BIBLE-BASED WORKBOOK

Take an adventure into the amazing Book of Mark and test your knowledge as you go!

PROJECT KINGDOM COME

THE BOOK OF
LUKE
BIBLE-BASED WORKBOOK

Take an adventure into the amazing Book of Luke and test your knowledge as you go!

PROJECT KINGDOM COME

THE BOOK OF
JOHN
BIBLE-BASED WORKBOOK

Take an adventure into the amazing Book of John and test your knowledge as you go!

PROJECT KINGDOM COME

THE BOOK OF
ACTS
BIBLE-BASED WORKBOOK

Take an adventure into the amazing Book of Acts and test your knowledge as you go!

PROJECT KINGDOM COME

THE BOOK OF
REVELATION
BIBLE-BASED WORKBOOK

Take an adventure into the amazing Book of Revelation and test your knowledge as you go!

PROJECT KINGDOM COME

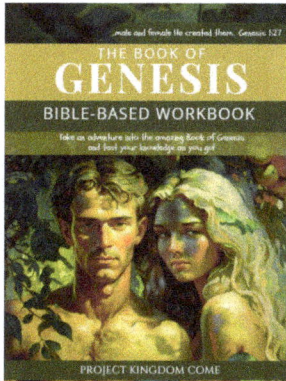

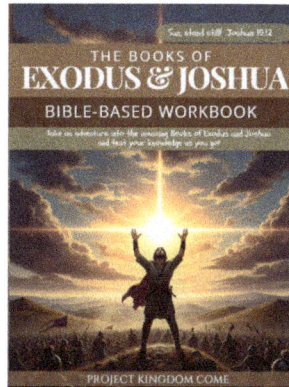

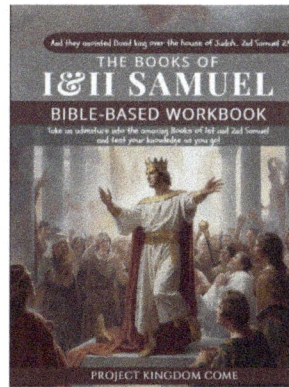

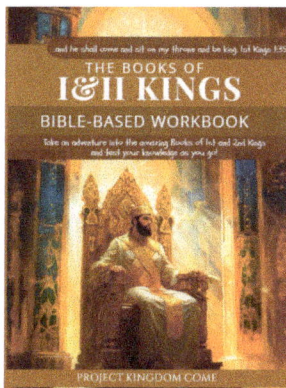

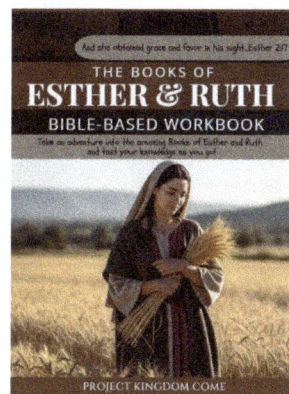

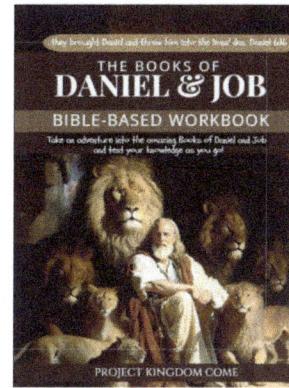

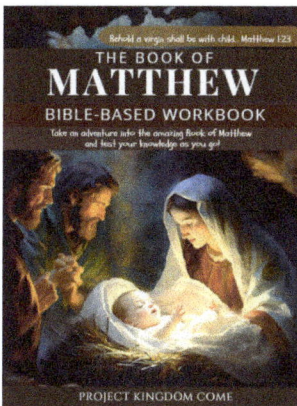

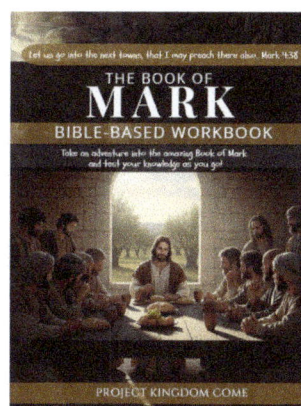

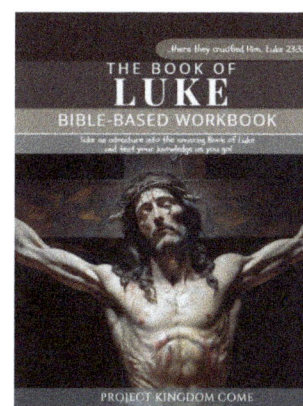

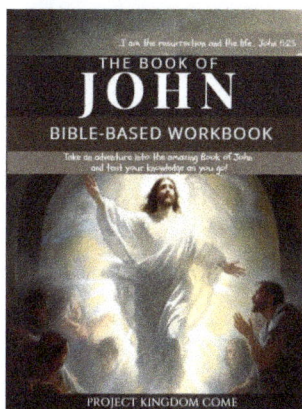

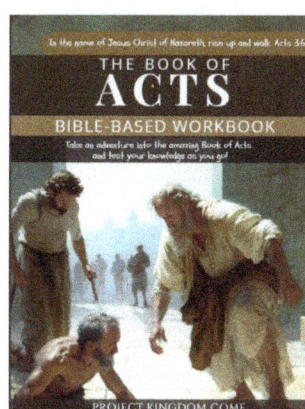

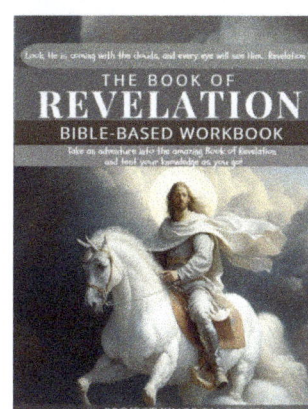

WWW.MYBIBLEWORKBOOKS.COM

PROJECT KINGDOM COME

This workbook belongs to:

_____

_____

_____

Leave your mark!

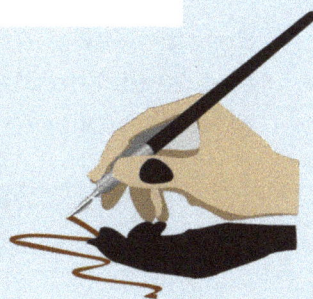

HOW TO USE THIS WORKBOOK

This workbook is designed to help young people explore the treasures in God's Word while having fun, growing in faith, and learning how to search the Scriptures for life's answers.

Here is what you will find inside:

Multiple Choice Questions
Each question comes directly from Scripture and includes a reference verse to help with locating the answer in the Bible. If possible, use a physical Bible to search for the answers.

Weekly Segments
Questions are grouped in weekly categories that could also be completed in a shorter or longer time frame.

Weekly Memory Verses
At the start of every week is a Bible verse to memorize. Each day of that week will repeat that memory verse with a chance to test memorization at the end of the week.

Certificate of Completion
At the end of the workbook, please find a Certificate of Achievement, ready for the child's name and parent or teacher's signature. Celebrate the accomplishment of studying an entire book in the Bible!

Answer Key
The workbook contains an answer key to serve as a support tool for parents or teachers reviewing the responses.

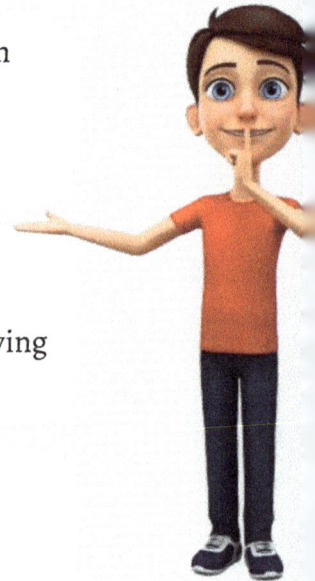

Recommendation for Parents and/or Teachers: Review the responses with your child or student and discuss lessons learned or interesting insights, to improve the child's retention and enrichment in the knowledge of God's word.

> You can do all things through Christ who gives you strength!
> Philippians 4:13

SAMPLE QUESTION...
HOW TO USE THIS WORKBOOK

Reading the reference verse will always lead you to the correct answer!

In the beginning was: (John 1:1)

A The Word
B. Heaven and Earth
C. Heaven only
D. Earth only

The number that comes after the book is the 'Chapter'

This is the name of a book in the Bible

John 1:1

The number after the chapter is the 'Verse'

NOW TEST YOURSELF! FIND JOSHUA CHAPTER 1 VERSE 8 IN YOUR BIBLE!

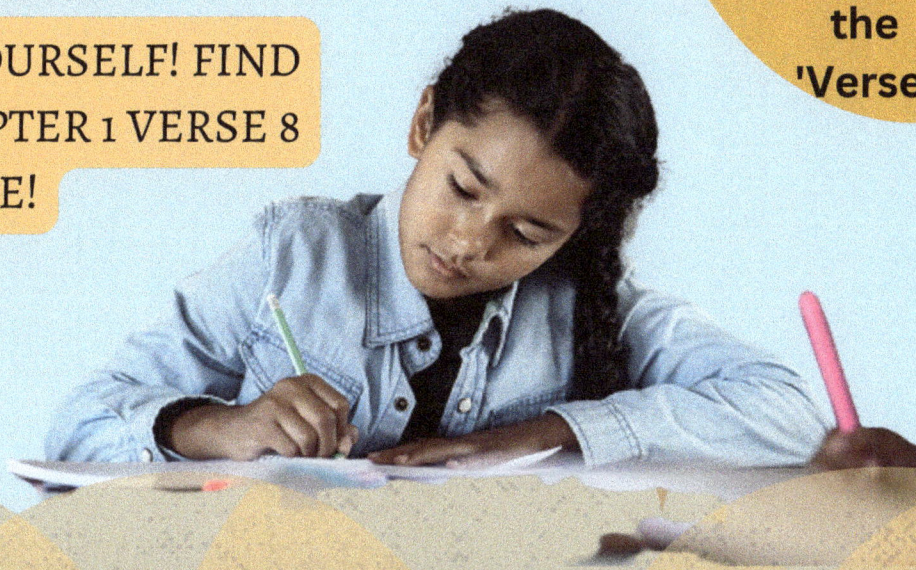

INTRODUCTION: THE BOOK OF MATTHEW

Discover Jesus, the Promised King and Savior of the World

The **Book of Matthew** is the first book in the New Testament, and it tells the amazing story of Jesus, the Son of God, the Messiah, and the King that God promised long ago. Written by **Matthew**, **a former tax collector turned disciple**, this Gospel shows us how Jesus fulfilled the Old Testament prophecies and brought God's kingdom to earth.

Through Matthew's eyes, we get to see **the life, teachings, miracles, death, and resurrection of Jesus.** We hear **the Sermon on the Mount**, watch **Jesus heal the sick** and **love the outcasts**, and **learn what it really means to follow Him.**

As you go through this workbook, you will discover:

- **Jesus is the long-awaited King and Savior**
- **God keeps His promises — every single one**
- **Jesus teaches us how to live with love, truth, and humility**
- **True greatness comes from serving others**
- **The Gospel is for everyone, and we are called to share it**

Matthew ends with a powerful command — **the Great Commission** — where Jesus tells His disciples to go into the world and make more disciples. That includes you, too!

So get ready to dive in, explore the Gospel, and meet the King of kings — Jesus!

"But seek first the kingdom of God and His righteousness, and all these things shall be added to you." - Matthew 6:33

WEEK 1

1. Mary became pregnant through the power of _____ (Matthew 1:18)

   A. God
   B. Wind
   C. Holy Spirit
   D. Fire

2. Why did Joseph consider quietly ending his engagement to Mary? (Matthew 1:18-19)

   A. He discovered she was pregnant before they were married
   B. He did not want to disgrace her publicly
   C. Both A and B
   D. He did not love her anymore

3. Why was the baby to be named Jesus? (Matthew 1:21)

   A. Jesus is a beautiful name
   B. Jesus was born at night
   C. He would save all the little children
   D. He would save His people from their sins

WEEK 1 MEMORY VERSE: MATTHEW 1:21
And she will bring forth a Son, and you shall call His name JESUS, for He will save His people from their sins.

WEEK 1

4. **What does the name Immanuel mean? (Matthew 1:23)**

A. Jesus is Lord
B. Christ the Savior
C. Savior of the world
D. God with us

5. **Mary was still a virgin when she conceived by the Holy Spirit. (Matthew 1:23)**

A. True
B. False

6. **In what City was Jesus born? (Matthew 2:1)**

A. Babylon
B. Bethlehem
C. Jerusalem
D. The City of God

WEEK 1 MEMORY VERSE: MATTHEW 1:21
And she will bring forth a Son, and you shall call His name JESUS, for
He will save His people from their sins.

WEEK 1

7.   Why were the wise men (Magi) looking for Jesus? (Matthew 2:1-2)

A. They saw His star and came to worship Him
B. An angel of the Lord led them to Jesus in order to worship Him
C. They were following King Herod's instructions
D. They came to pray for Baby Jesus

8.   What gifts did the wise men bring to Jesus? (Matthew 2:11)

A. Myrrh
B. Gold
C. Frankincense
D. All the above

9.   Why did the angel warn Joseph in a dream to flee from Bethlehem? (Matthew 2:13)

A. The wise men were looking for Jesus
B. King Herod wanted to worship Jesus
C. King Herod wanted to kill Jesus
D. The wise men would tell Herod where Jesus was

WEEK 1 MEMORY VERSE: MATTHEW 1:21
And she will bring forth a Son, and you shall call His name JESUS, for
He will save His people from their sins.

WEEK 1

10. **Where did Joseph take Mary and Jesus after fleeing Bethlehem? (Matthew 2:13)**

A. Jerusalem
B. Egypt
C. The City of David
D. The City of God

11. **Why did King Herod kill all boys in Bethlehem two years old and under? (Matthew 2:16)**

A. He knew Jesus was under two years old
B. He wanted Jesus to be among the boys that were killed
C. He was angry that the wise men had tricked him
D. All the above

12. **Why did Joseph decide to live in Nazareth instead of going back to Judea? (Matthew 2:22-23)**

A. Because Bethlehem was too far
B. Because an angel told him to go there
C. Because Herod's son was ruling in Judea
D. Because the wise men had warned him

WEEK 1 MEMORY VERSE: MATTHEW 1:21

And she will bring forth a Son, and you shall call His name JESUS, for He will save His people from their sins.

WEEK 1

13.   **Which of the following is true concerning John the Baptist? (Matthew 3:1-11)**

A. He prepared the way for Jesus
B. He preached repentance
C. He baptized people with water for repentance
D. All the above

14.   **Who was John the Baptist referring to when he spoke of someone mightier coming after him? (Matthew 3:11)**

A. Jesus
B. The Sadducees
C. The Pharisees
D. Prophet Isaiah

15.   **According to John, Jesus will baptize with _____ (Matthew 3:11)**

A. Water
B. The Holy Spirit and with fire
C. Oil
D. Prayers

WEEK 1 MEMORY VERSE: MATTHEW 1:21
And she will bring forth a Son, and you shall call His name JESUS, for He will save His people from their sins.

**16. What did John say when Jesus came to be baptized?
(Matthew 3:13–14)**

A. John felt Jesus should baptize him instead
B. John had to baptize Jesus in order to fulfill prophecy
C. John felt unworthy to baptize Jesus
D. All the above

17. What happened after Jesus was baptized? (Matthew 3:16-17)

A. The heavens were opened
B. The Spirit of God descended upon Him in the form of a dove
C. A voice from heaven said, "This is my beloved Son, with whom I am well pleased"
D. All the above

**18. How did Jesus respond when tempted to turn stones to bread?
(Matthew 4:3-4)**

A. You shall not put the Lord your God to the test
B. You shall worship the Lord your God, and He only shall you serve
C. Man shall not live by bread alone but by every word that proceeds from the mouth of the Lord
D. Jesus did not respond

WEEK 1 MEMORY VERSE: MATTHEW 1:21
And she will bring forth a Son, and you shall call His name JESUS, for He will save His people from their sins.

19. **What was Jesus' response to: "If you are the Son of God, throw yourself down"? (Matthew 4:5-7)**

A. You shall not put the Lord your God to the test
B. You shall worship the Lord your God, and He only shall you serve
C. Man shall not live by bread alone but by every word that proceeds from the mouth of the Lord
D. Jesus did not respond

20. **How did Jesus respond to: "I will give you all the kingdoms of the world if only you would fall down and worship me"? (Matthew 4:8-10)**

A. You shall not put the Lord your God to the test
B. You shall worship the Lord your God, and He only shall you serve
C. Man shall not live by bread alone but by every word that proceeds from the mouth of the Lord
D. Jesus did not respond

21. **What happened after the devil left Jesus in the wilderness? (Matthew 4:11)**

A. Jesus continued to fast and pray
B. The angels came and ministered to Jesus
C. Jesus thanked God for giving Him victory
D. Jesus immediately began preaching to the crowds

WEEK 1 MEMORY VERSE: MATTHEW 1:21
And she will bring forth a Son, and you shall call His name JESUS, for He will save His people from their sins.

"

I can do all things through Christ that gives me strength (Philippians 4:13)

"

Great job completing the week!

Did you memorize the daily verse?
Test yourself by writing it here...

_____

_____

_____

_____

_____

Use this space to draw a scene from the Bible or reflect on something you learned, felt or experienced...

WEEK 2

22. **What did Jesus do when He heard John the Baptist had been arrested? (Matthew 4:12)**

A. He went to Bethlehem
B. He withdrew to Galilee
C. He began to pray for John
D. He planned to help John escape

23. **What did Jesus say to Simon (Peter) and Andrew when He called them? (Matthew 4:19)**

A. Follow me, and I will make you fishers of men
B. Follow me, and I will show you how to prosper
C. Leave your father and mother and follow me
D. Give up everything and follow me

24. **What were James and John doing when Jesus called them? (Matthew 4:21)**

A. They were with their father Zebedee
B. They were mending their fishing nets
C. Both A and B
D. They were preaching

WEEK 2 MEMORY VERSE: MATTHEW 5:16
Let your light so shine before men, that they may see your good works and glorify your Father in heaven.

WEEK 2

25. **What did the ministry of Jesus consist of? (Matthew 4:23-24)**

A. Teaching and preaching the Good News
B. Healing all kinds of diseases and afflictions
C. Healing those oppressed by demons
D. All the above

26. **Blessed are the poor in Spirit (Matthew 5:3)**

A. For they shall inherit the earth
B. For they shall be filled
C. For theirs is the kingdom of heaven
D. For they shall be called sons of God

27. **Blessed are the meek (Matthew 5:5)**

A. For great is their reward in heaven
B. For they shall inherit the earth
C. For they shall obtain mercy
D. For they shall see God

WEEK 2 MEMORY VERSE: MATTHEW 5:16
Let your light so shine before men, that they may see your
good works and glorify your Father in heaven.

WEEK 2

28. **Blessed are those who hunger and thirst for righteousness (Matthew 5:6)**

A. For they shall inherit the earth
B. For they shall be filled
C. For theirs is the kingdom of heaven
D. For they shall be called sons of God

29. **Blessed are the peacemakers (Matthew 5:9)**

A. For they shall inherit the earth
B. For they shall be filled
C. For theirs is the kingdom of heaven
D. For they shall be called sons of God

30. **Blessed are those who are persecuted for righteousness' sake (Matthew 5:10)**

A. For they shall inherit the earth
B. For they shall be filled
C. For theirs is the kingdom of heaven
D. For they shall be called sons of God

WEEK 2 MEMORY VERSE: MATTHEW 5:16

Let your light so shine before men, that they may see your good works and glorify your Father in heaven.

WEEK 2

31. Blessed are you when people insult you and persecute you falsely for Jesus' sake (Matthew 5:11-12)

A. For great is your reward in heaven
B. For you shall inherit the earth
C. For you shall obtain mercy
D. For you shall see God

32. Jesus compared believers to …. (Matthew 5:13-14)

A. The salt and the light of the world
B. Blessings
C. Doers of righteousness
D. The merciful

33. Why does Jesus say we should let our light shine? (Matthew 5:16)

A. So we can be like stars
B. So people will see our good works and glorify God
C. So we can have peaceful lives
D. So we are rewarded for our mercy

WEEK 2 MEMORY VERSE: MATTHEW 5:16
Let your light so shine before men, that they may see your good works and glorify your Father in heaven.

WEEK 2

34. **Jesus did not come to destroy the law or the prophets but to?**
(Matthew 5:17)

A. Expose them
B. Teach them
C. Fulfill them
D. Make them better

35. **Who will be called great or least in the kingdom of heaven?**
(Matthew 5:19)

A. Those who break commandments and teach others to do the same = least
B. Those who obey and teach the commandments = great
C. Those who try their best will be great
D. Both A and B

36. **Which of the following did Jesus say is the same as murdering your brother? (Matthew 5:21-22)**

A. Gossip
B. Anger
C. Anger without cause
D. Insulting others

WEEK 2 MEMORY VERSE: MATTHEW 5:16
Let your light so shine before men, that they may see your good works and glorify your Father in heaven.

WEEK 2

37. What did Jesus say is the same as looking at a woman with lust?
(Matthew 5:27-28)

A. Murder
B. Adultery
C. Idolatry
D. None of the above

38. Why did Jesus say to pluck out your right eye if it causes you to sin?
(Matthew 5:29)

A. Because you have two eyes and can use the other eye
B. Because it is better that you lose one part of your body than for your whole body to be thrown into hell
C. The devil is using your eyes
D. Jesus didn't say that

39. What did Jesus say we should do instead of swearing oaths?
(Matthew 5:33-37)

A. Swear by your own head
B. Swear by heaven
C. Swear by the earth
D. Let your "Yes" be "Yes," and your "No," "No"

WEEK 2 MEMORY VERSE: MATTHEW 5:16

Let your light so shine before men, that they may see your good works and glorify your Father in heaven.

WEEK 2

40. If someone slaps your right cheek, what should you do? (Matthew 5:39)

A. Don't slap them
B. Pray for them
C. Ignore them
D. Turn the other cheek to them also

41. Do not resist an evil person. If someone slaps you on your right cheek, offer the other cheek also (Mathew 5:39)

A. True
B. False

42. Which of the following statements is NOT found in the Bible? (Matthew 5:40-42)

A. If someone sues you for your tunic, give them your cloak also
B. Go the second mile when compelled to go one
C. Give to those who ask; don't turn away borrowers
D. Stand your ground when you are provoked

WEEK 2 MEMORY VERSE: MATTHEW 5:16
Let your light so shine before men, that they may see your good works and glorify your Father in heaven.

"

Oh Lord you are my God.
Earnestly I seek You,
my soul thirsts for You
(Psalm 63:1)

"

Great job completing the week!

**Did you memorize the daily verse?
Test yourself by writing it here...**

_____

_____

_____

_____

_____

**Use this space to draw a scene from the Bible or reflect
on something you learned, felt or experienced...**

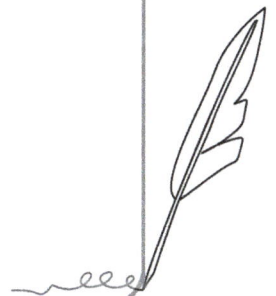

WEEK 3

43. What did Jesus say to do instead of hating your enemies?
(Matthew 5:44)

A. Love your enemies and bless those who curse you
B. Do good to those who hate you
C. Pray for those who spitefully use you and persecute you
D. All the above

44. Why should we love our enemies? (Matthew 5:44-48)

A. That we may be sons of our Father in heaven
B. Because God blesses both the righteous and the wicked
C. So we may be perfect as our Father in heaven is perfect
D. All the above

45. What did Jesus teach about doing good deeds?
(Matthew 6:1-4)

A. Do them to please God, not people
B. Don't let your left hand know what your right hand is doing
C. Do them in secret—God sees and rewards openly
D. All the above

WEEK 3 MEMORY VERSE: MATTHEW 6:33
But seek first the kingdom of God and His righteousness, and all these things shall be added to you.

WEEK 3

46. **What did Jesus teach about prayer? (Matthew 6:5-6)**

A. Do not be like hypocrites who love public prayers in order to be seen by others
B. Pray privately—go into your room and shut the door
C. God sees in secret and rewards openly
D. All the above

47. **Which of these lines is NOT part of the Lord's Prayer?**
(Matthew 6:9-13)

A. Hallowed be Your name. Your kingdom come...
B. Give us this day our daily bread...
C. Deliver us from the evil one...
D. Now I lay me down to sleep...

48. **Why must we forgive others? (Matthew 6:14-15)**

A. Because they asked us to
B. Because we want to be merciful
C. So we can be like God
D. So our Father in heaven will also forgive us

WEEK 3 MEMORY VERSE: MATTHEW 6:33
But seek first the kingdom of God and His righteousness, and all these things shall be added to you.

WEEK 3

49. **What did Jesus teach about fasting? (Matthew 6:16-18)**

A. Don't look gloomy to show others you are fasting
B. Anoint your head and wash your face
C. Fast in secret—God sees and rewards you
D. All the above

50. **What did Jesus say about where your treasure is? (Matthew 6:19-21)**

A. It will be safe in heaven
B. There, your heart will be also
C. There your mind will be also
D. All the above

51. **To what does Jesus compare the eye? (Matthew 6:22)**

A. The lamp of the body
B. The light of the body
C. A candle
D. A fire

WEEK 3 MEMORY VERSE: MATTHEW 6:33
But seek first the kingdom of God and His righteousness, and all these things shall be added to you.

WEEK 3

52.   What did Jesus say are the two masters that no one can serve at the same time? (Matthew 6:24)

A. God and Satan
B. God and man
C. God and yourself
D. God and money (mammon)

53.   Why did Jesus tell us not to worry? (Matthew 6:25-30)

A. Because God feeds the birds and we are more valuable
B. Because God clothes the lilies and we are worth more
C. Because worry adds nothing to our lives
D. All the above

54.   What did Jesus say to seek first instead of worrying? (Matthew 6:31-33)

A. Being righteous
B. Getting to heaven
C. Praying and reading the word of God
D. Seeking the kingdom of God and His righteousness above all else, and all these other things will be added to us

WEEK 3 MEMORY VERSE: MATTHEW 6:33
But seek first the kingdom of God and His righteousness, and all these things shall be added to you.

WEEK 3

55. Finish this verse: "Do not worry about tomorrow _____"
(Matthew 6:34)

A. For tomorrow is not promised
B. For God will take care of tomorrow
C. For tomorrow will be anxious for itself.
D. For God holds the future

56. Why did Jesus caution us not to judge others? (Matthew 7:1-2)

A. That we, too, may not be judged
B. Because the measure we use will be used on us
C. Because we are not God
D. Both A and B

57. Why did Jesus say to remove the plank from your own eye first??
(Matthew 7:3-5)

A. So you can see clearly enough to help your brother
B. So that others will think you are humble
C. Because the plank is heavier than the speck
D. Because judging others is always wrong

WEEK 3 MEMORY VERSE: MATTHEW 6:33
But seek first the kingdom of God and His righteousness, and all these things shall be added to you.

WEEK 3

58. Why should you not give what is holy to the dogs or throw pearls to pigs? (Matthew 7:6)

A. They will trample them under their feet, then turn and tear you to pieces
B. Because animals cannot receive spiritual truths
C. Because dogs and pigs are unclean animals
D. All the above

59. What does Jesus say about asking, seeking, and knocking? (Matthew 7:7)

A. You will get what you ask for, find what you seek, and the door will be opened to you
B. You will be told to wait and try again
C. You might get what you want if you ask enough times
D. Only some people will receive answers when they pray

60. How did Jesus prove that God gives good gifts to those who ask Him? (Matthew 7:8-11)

A. A father doesn't give stones when asked for bread
B. A father doesn't give a serpent when asked for a fish
C. If earthly fathers know how to give good gifts, how much more our Father in heaven
D. All the above

WEEK 3 MEMORY VERSE: MATTHEW 6:33
But seek first the kingdom of God and His righteousness, and all these things shall be added to you.

WEEK 3

61. Complete this teaching of Jesus "Do unto others _____" (Matthew 7:12)

A. As you would want them to do to you
B. As commanded in the Bible
C. The right thing always
D. Good so that you will not be judged

62. Why does Jesus say to enter by the narrow gate? (Matthew 7:13-14)

A. The wide gate leads to destruction and many enter through it
B. The narrow gate leads to life, and few find it
C. The pearly heavenly gate is narrow
D. Both A and B

63. How will we recognize false prophets? (Matthew 7:15-20)

A. By their fruits (deeds/actions)
B. By how well they prophesy
C. By how well they preach
D. By the miracles they perform

WEEK 3 MEMORY VERSE: MATTHEW 6:33
But seek first the kingdom of God and His righteousness, and all these things shall be added to you.

"
I lay down and slept;
I awoke for the Lord
sustained me
(Psalm 3:5)
"

Great job completing the week!

Did you memorize the daily verse?
Test yourself by writing it here...

_____

_____

_____

_____

_____

_____

Use this space to draw a scene from the Bible or reflect
on something you learned, felt or experienced...

WEEK 4

64. Who did Jesus say will enter the kingdom of heaven?
(Matthew 7:21-23)

A. Those who say "Lord, Lord"
B. Those who perform miracles in His name
C. Those who do the will of the Father in heaven
D. All the above

65. Those who hear the word of God and act on it are like what?
(Matthew 7:24-25)

A. A wise man who builds his house on the rock
B. Three wise men
C. The wisdom of King Solomon
D. The wisdom that is not of this world

66. Those who hear the word of God and do not act on it are like what?
(Matthew 7:26-27)

A. A foolish man who built his house on sand
B. The foolishness of the devil
C. The deceitfulness of the serpent
D. Darkness and confusion

WEEK 4 MEMORY VERSE: MATTHEW 7:7
Ask, and it will be given to you; seek, and you will find; knock, and it will be opened to you.

WEEK 4

67. **Why were the crowds amazed at Jesus' teaching? (Matthew 7:28-29)**

A. He taught in parables
B. He had great insight
C. He taught with authority, not like the scribes
D. He said things they had never heard before

68. **What did Jesus do when the leper said, 'Lord, if You are willing, You can make me clean'? (Matthew 8:1-4)**

A. Jesus touched him and said, "I am willing. Be cleansed."
B. He asked him to tell no one
C. He told him to go show himself to the priest
D. All the above

69. **Why did the Centurion tell Jesus not to come to his house to heal his servant? (Matthew 8:5–8)**

A. He felt unworthy for Jesus to go to his house
B. He believed Jesus could heal by just saying the word
C. He believed Jesus had the authority to command sickness out of his servant without being physically present
D. All the above

WEEK 4 MEMORY VERSE: MATTHEW 7:7
Ask, and it will be given to you; seek, and you will find; knock, and it will be opened to you.

WEEK 4

70. **What did Jesus say about the Centurion's faith? (Matthew 8:10-12)**

A. He had not seen such faith with anyone in Israel
B. Jesus was amazed at the love the Centurion had for his servant
C. Jesus was amazed at how much authority the Centurion had in Capernaum
D. All the above

71. **What did Jesus say about His meeting with the Centurion? (Matthew 8:10-13)**

A. Many will come from the east and west and sit with Abraham, Isaac, and Jacob in the kingdom
B. The sons of the kingdom will be cast out into outer darkness
C. Both A and B
D. Jesus did not respond

72. **What prophecy was fulfilled when Jesus healed the sick and cast out demons? (Matthew 8:17)**

A. He will have the authority to heal the sick and cast out demons
B. All power and authority was given to Jesus
C. He Himself took our infirmities and bore our sicknesses
D. Jesus is both Lord and lamb

WEEK 4 MEMORY VERSE: MATTHEW 7:7
Ask, and it will be given to you; seek, and you will find; knock, and it will be opened to you.

WEEK 4

73.   **What did Jesus say to the scribe who said he would follow Him anywhere? (Matthew 8:19–20)**

A. Foxes have holes, and birds of the air have nests, but the Son of Man has nowhere to lay his head
B. Take up your cross and follow me
C. Follow me, and I will make you a fisher of men
D. I am the way, the truth, and the life

74.   **What did Jesus say to the disciple who wanted to first go bury his father? (Matthew 8:21–22)**

A. If you want to follow me, you must first forget about yourself
B. Deny yourself and follow Me
C. I am the way, the truth, and the life
D. Follow me and let the dead bury their own dead

75.   **What happened when a storm arose while Jesus and His disciples were on the boat? (Matthew 8:23–27)**

A. The disciples panicked and woke Jesus
B. Jesus rebuked the wind and waves
C. The disciples marveled that even the winds obey Jesus
D. All the above

WEEK 4 MEMORY VERSE: MATTHEW 7:7
Ask, and it will be given to you; seek, and you will find; knock, and it will be opened to you.

WEEK 4

76. Which of the following did NOT happen when Jesus met the demon-possessed men in Gergesenes? (Matthew 8:28–34)

A. The demons asked Jesus if He came to torment them
B. The demons were cast into pigs who rushed into the sea
C. The town begged Jesus to leave
D. Jesus prayed for the men's families

77. Why did the scribes accuse Jesus of blasphemy after He healed the paralyzed man? (Matthew 9:1–6)

A. Because He claimed to be able to forgive sins
B. Because He claimed to heal the sick
C. Because He claimed to have power
D. Because He claimed to be God

78. What was Jesus' response when questioned about eating with sinners? (Matthew 9:12–13)

A. Those who are well do not need a doctor, sick people do
B. I desire mercy and not sacrifice
C. I did not come to call the righteous but sinners to repentance
D. All the above

WEEK 4 MEMORY VERSE: MATTHEW 7:7

Ask, and it will be given to you; seek, and you will find; knock, and it will be opened to you.

WEEK 4

79. How did Jesus respond when asked why His disciples didn't fast?
(Matthew 9:14–17)

A. The friends of the bridegroom don't fast while He's with them
B. New cloth shouldn't be patched onto old garments
C. New wine must go into new wineskins
D. All the above

80. Why did the woman with the issue of blood touch Jesus' garment?
(Matthew 9:20-21)

A. She hoped to get His attention
B. She believed she would get healed if she touched the hem of His garment
C. She wanted to speak with Him
D. She wanted Him to come to her home

81. Why did the crowd laugh at Jesus when He arrived at Jairus' house?
(Matthew 9:23-24)

A. Because Jesus had told them that the girl was not dead but sleeping
B. They hated Jesus
C. They thought Jesus was a blasphemer
D. All the above

WEEK 4 MEMORY VERSE: MATTHEW 7:7
Ask, and it will be given to you; seek, and you will find; knock, and it will be opened to you.

WEEK 4

82. What did Jesus do when two blind men cried, "Son of David, have mercy on us"? (Matthew 9:27–31)

A. He asked if they believed He could heal them
B. He touched their eyes and healed them
C. He told them not to tell anyone
D. All the above

83. What did the Pharisees accuse Jesus of after He healed the mute, demon-possessed man? (Matthew 9:32–34)

A. Blasphemy
B. Leading people astray
C. Using demonic power to cast out demons
D. Claiming to be God

84. What did Jesus say after seeing the crowds, describing them as weary and scattered like sheep without a shepherd? (Matthew 9:36–38)

A. "The harvest truly is plentiful, but the laborers are few."
B. "Therefore pray the Lord of the harvest to send out laborers into His harvest."
C. He told the disciples to go out and heal them immediately
D. Both A and B

WEEK 4 MEMORY VERSE: MATTHEW 7:7
Ask, and it will be given to you; seek, and you will find; knock, and it will be opened to you.

"

I rejoice in the Lord
always
(Philippians 4:4)

"

Great job completing the week!

Did you memorize the daily verse?
Test yourself by writing it here...

_____

_____

_____

_____

_____

_____

Use this space to draw a scene from the Bible or reflect on something you learned, felt or experienced...

WEEK 5

85. Jesus gave His disciples power over unclean spirits, to cast them out, and to heal all kinds of sicknesses and all kinds of diseases (Matthew 10:1)

A. True
B. False

86. How many disciples did Jesus appoint? (Matthew 10:2)

A. 5
B. 7
C. 11
D. 12

87. Which of the following was not one of Jesus' disciples? (Matthew 10:2-4)

A. Andrew
B. Matthew
C. Luke
D. Simon

WEEK 5 MEMORY VERSE: MATTHEW 16:26

For what profit is it to a man if he gains the whole world, and loses his own soul? Or what will a man give in exchange for his soul?

WEEK 5

88. **Where did Jesus tell the disciples to go when He first sent them out? (Matthew 10:5–6)**

A. To the lost sheep of the house of Israel
B. To the sick
C. To the oppressed
D. To the poor

89. **Jesus told His disciples, "Freely you have received, _____." (Matthew 10:8)**

A. Be grateful
B. Pray for others
C. Freely give
D. Feed my sheep

90. **Why did Jesus tell the disciples not to take money or supplies when He sent them out? (Matthew 10:9–10)**

A. Those who work deserve to be provided for
B. Jesus didn't want them to get tired
C. He wanted them to fast
D. He wanted them to suffer

WEEK 5 MEMORY VERSE: MATTHEW 16:26

For what profit is it to a man if he gains the whole world, and loses his own soul? Or what will a man give in exchange for his soul?

WEEK 5

91. What did Jesus tell the disciples to do if a household was not worthy? (Matthew 10:11–14)

A. Let your peace return to you
B. Shake the dust off your feet when you leave
C. Don't stay with them
D. All the above

92. Jesus said, "I send you out as sheep among wolves." What was His caution? (Matthew 10:16)

A. Be wise as serpents and harmless as doves
B. Be strong and courageous
C. Trust the Holy Spirit
D. Be not afraid

93. Why did Jesus tell the disciples not to worry when arrested? (Matthew 10:17–20)

A. God would give them the right words to speak at the right time
B. It is not them who will be speaking
C. It is the Holy Spirit who will be speaking through them
D. All the above

WEEK 5 MEMORY VERSE: MATTHEW 16:26
For what profit is it to a man if he gains the whole world, and loses his own soul? Or what will a man give in exchange for his soul?

WEEK 5

94. What did Jesus say would happen to those who endure to the end? (Matthew 10:22)

A. They would be saved
B. They would inherit the kingdom of God
C. They would see God
D. They will receive mercy

95. What were the disciples cautioned to do if they were persecuted in one City? (Matthew 10:23)

A. Hide and Pray
B. Find a safe house
C. Flee to the next city
D. All the above

96. What are some of the reasons Jesus told His disciples not to fear? (Matthew 10:25-31)

A. If they called Jesus evil, they will call you worse
B. Fear God who can destroy both soul and body
C. You are valuable to God—He knows every hair on your head
D. All the above

WEEK 5 MEMORY VERSE: MATTHEW 16:26

For what profit is it to a man if he gains the whole world, and loses his own soul? Or what will a man give in exchange for his soul?

WEEK 5

97. What will Jesus do if we confess Him before others?
(Matthew 10:32)

A. He will bless us
B. He will confess us before His Father
C. He will give us a long life
D. He will strengthen us

98. What did Jesus mean when He said He did not come to the earth to bring peace but a sword? (Matthew 10:34-39)

A. He who loves his father or mother more than Him is not worthy of Him
B. He who does not take his cross and follow Jesus is not worthy of Him
C. He who finds his life would lose it, and he who loses his life for Christ's sake would find it
D. All the above

99. What reward will someone receive for honoring a righteous man?
(Matthew 10:40-41)

A. A righteous man's reward
B. A prophet's reward
C. Both A and B
D. This is not in the Bible

WEEK 5 MEMORY VERSE: MATTHEW 16:26

For what profit is it to a man if he gains the whole world, and loses his own soul? Or what will a man give in exchange for his soul?

WEEK 5

100. How did Jesus answer John's question about being the Messiah? (Matthew 11:2-5)

A. Yes, I am the One
B. The blind see, the lame walk, and the lepers are cleansed
C. "You shall know the truth, and it shall set you free"
D. All the above

101. What did Jesus say about John the Baptist? (Matthew 11:7-14)

A. He is more than a prophet; he was sent to prepare the way for Jesus
B. Among those born of a woman, none is greater than John the Baptist, yet he who is least in the kingdom of heaven is greater than he
C. He is Elijah who is to come
D. All the above

102. Jesus said that from the days of John the Baptist until now, the kingdom of heaven suffers violence and .... (Matthew 11:12)

A. The violent shall be destroyed
B. The violent take it by force
C. The peacemakers shall inherit the kingdom of God
D. The peacemakers shall be called the children of God

WEEK 5 MEMORY VERSE: MATTHEW 16:26

For what profit is it to a man if he gains the whole world, and loses his own soul? Or what will a man give in exchange for his soul?

WEEK 5

103.   What did people say about John and Jesus regarding eating and drinking? (Matthew 11:18–19)

A. John has a demon; Jesus is a glutton and friend of sinners
B. John is a loner; Jesus doesn't fast
C. John is strange; Jesus is too social
D. John is possessed; Jesus breaks tradition

104.   Who did Jesus say can truly know the Father? (Matthew 11:27)

A. Those who read the Word of God
B. Those who follow Jesus Christ
C. Those to whom the Son chooses to reveal Him
D. Those who are born again

105.   What does Jesus offer to the weary and heavy-laden? (Matthew 11:28)

A. Rest
B. Healing
C. Comfort
D. Strength

WEEK 5 MEMORY VERSE: MATTHEW 16:26

For what profit is it to a man if he gains the whole world, and loses his own soul? Or what will a man give in exchange for his soul?

Open my eyes that I may see the wondrous things from Your law (Psalm 119:18)

Great job completing the week!

Did you memorize the daily verse?
Test yourself by writing it here...

_____

_____

_____

_____

_____

_____

Use this space to draw a scene from the Bible or reflect
on something you learned, felt or experienced...

WEEK 6

106. Why does Jesus tell us to take His yoke and learn from Him? (Matthew 11:28-30)

A. His yoke is easy, and his burden is light
B. He is a great teacher
C. He is a mighty deliverer
D. He is the greatest comforter

107. How did Jesus respond to complaints about His disciples picking grain on the Sabbath? (Matthew 12:1–8)

A. David ate the holy bread
B. The Son of Man is Lord of the Sabbath
C. God desires mercy, not sacrifice
D. All the above

108. What did Jesus say when asked if healing on the Sabbath was lawful? (Matthew 12:10–12)

A. Jesus did not respond
B. Jesus told them to read the Bible
C. He asked if they would save a sheep on the Sabbath and said people are more valuable
D. He told them not to worry

WEEK 6 MEMORY VERSE: MATTHEW 17:20

for assuredly, I say to you, if you have faith as a mustard seed, you will say to this mountain, 'Move from here to there,' and it will move; and nothing will be impossible for you.

WEEK 6

109. What did the Pharisees say after Jesus healed a demon-possessed blind and mute man? (Matthew 12:22–24)

A. They wondered whether He was the Son of David
B. They said He was casting out demons using demonic powers
C. Both A and B
D. The Pharisees did not say anything

110. Jesus said, "He who is not with Me _____ and he who does not gather with Me _____ (Matthew 12:30)

A. Is not worthy of the kingdom of God - gathers in vain
B. Is not worthy to be called a Child of God - gathers in vain
C. Is against me - scatters abroad
D. Is against the one who sent me - scatters abroad

111. What sin did Jesus say would not be forgiven? (Matthew 12:31-32)

A. Blasphemy against the Holy Spirit
B. Blasphemy against the Father
C. Blasphemy against the Son
D. Denying the Trinity

WEEK 6 MEMORY VERSE: MATTHEW 17:20

for assuredly, I say to you, if you have faith as a mustard seed, you will say to this mountain, 'Move from here to there,' and it will move; and nothing will be impossible for you.

WEEK 6

112. Which of the following is NOT something Jesus taught about fruit and the heart? (Matthew 12:33–35)

A. Good trees bear good fruit; bad trees bear bad fruit
B. The mouth speaks from the heart's overflow
C. A good man brings forth good from his treasure
D. Good fruits are hard to find

113. What did Jesus say about idle words? (Matthew 12:36–37)

A. We will give an account for them
B. Words will justify or condemn us
C. Both A and B
D. Say only nice things

114. Why did Jesus say the sign of Jonah would be the only sign given? (Matthew 12:38-42)

A. Jonah's preaching led to repentance, but Jesus was ignored
B. The Queen of Sheba sought Solomon's wisdom, but Jesus was rejected
C. Both A and B
D. Because Jesus didn't give signs

WEEK 6 MEMORY VERSE: MATTHEW 17:20

for assuredly, I say to you, if you have faith as a mustard seed, you will say to this mountain, 'Move from here to there,' and it will move; and nothing will be impossible for you.

WEEK 6

115. What did Jesus teach about unclean spirits returning to a person? (Matthew 12:43-45)

A. When they leave a man, they seek rest but find none, so they return
B. They return with seven other worse spirits
C. The final state of that man is worse than it was before
D. All the above

116. Who did Jesus say is His true family? (Matthew 12:46-50)

A. His disciples
B. Whoever does the will of His Father in heaven
C. His neighbors
D. Mary and James

117. What happened to the seed that fell by the wayside? (Mathew 13:3-4)

A. This seed was choked by thorns
B. The birds came and devoured this seed
C. This seed yielded a crop
D. This seed withered away because it had no root

WEEK 6 MEMORY VERSE: MATTHEW 17:20

for assuredly, I say to you, if you have faith as a mustard seed, you will say to this mountain, 'Move from here to there,' and it will move; and nothing will be impossible for you.

WEEK 6

118. What happened to the seed that fell on rocky ground?
(Mathew 13:5-6)

A. This seed was choked by thorns
B. The birds came and devoured this seed
C. This seed yielded a crop
D. This seed withered away because it had no root

119. What happened to the seed that fell among thorns? (Mathew 13:7)

A. This seed was choked by thorns
B. The birds came and devoured this seed
C. This seed yielded a crop
D. This seed withered away because it had no root

120. What was the result of seed that landed on good ground?
(Mathew 13:8)

A. This seed was choked by thorns
B. The birds came and devoured this seed
C. This seed yielded a crop
D. This seed withered away because it had no root

WEEK 6 MEMORY VERSE: MATTHEW 17:20

for assuredly, I say to you, if you have faith as a mustard seed, you will say to this mountain, 'Move from here to there,' and it will move; and nothing will be impossible for you.

WEEK 6

121. Why did Jesus speak in parables? (Matthew 13:10-15)

A. Because the mysteries of the kingdom are revealed to some but not to others
B. Those who listen will gain more understanding; those who don't will lose even what they have
C. Because people see but do not perceive, hear but do not understand
D. All the above

122. What does the seed by the wayside represent? (Matthew 13:19)

A. Those who hear but don't understand; the enemy snatches the word from their hearts
B. Those who receive the word with joy but fall away when problems arise
C. Those who understand and bear fruit
D. Those who are choked by riches and cares of life

123. What does the seed on stony ground represent? (Matthew 13:20-21)

A. Those who hear but don't understand; the enemy snatches the word from their hearts
B. Those who receive the word with joy but fall away when problems arise
C. Those who understand and bear fruit
D. Those who are choked by riches and cares of life

WEEK 6 MEMORY VERSE: MATTHEW 17:20

for assuredly, I say to you, if you have faith as a mustard seed, you will say to this mountain, 'Move from here to there,' and it will move; and nothing will be impossible for you.

WEEK 6

124. What does the seed among thorns represent? (Matthew 13:22)

A. Those who hear but don't understand; the enemy snatches the word from their hearts
B. Those who receive the word with joy but fall away when problems arise
C. Those who understand and bear fruit
D. Those who are choked by riches and cares of life

125. What does the seed on good ground represent? (Matthew 13:23)

A. Those who hear but don't understand; the enemy snatches the word from their hearts
B. Those who receive the word with joy but fall away when problems arise
C. Those who understand and bear fruit
D. Those who are choked by riches and cares of life

126. What did the farmer do to the wheat and the tares in the parable? (Matthew 13:24-30)

A. He pulled out the tares from the wheat
B. He let both the tares and wheat grow together until harvest
C. He separated the wheat from the tares then burned the tares but stored the wheat
D. Both B and C

WEEK 6 MEMORY VERSE: MATTHEW 17:20

for assuredly, I say to you, if you have faith as a mustard seed, you will say to this mountain, 'Move from here to there,' and it will move; and nothing will be impossible for you.

I shall lay up gold as dust, and the gold of Ophir as the stones of the brooks

(Job 22:24)

Great job completing the week!

Did you memorize the daily verse?
Test yourself by writing it here...

_____

_____

_____

_____

_____

Use this space to draw a scene from the Bible or reflect on something you learned, felt or experienced...

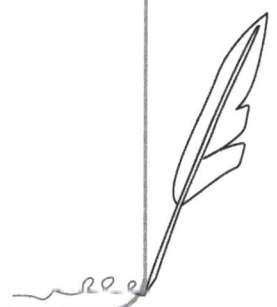

WEEK 7

127. What does the mustard seed teach about the kingdom of heaven? (Matthew 13:31-32)

A. It is like a mustard seed which is the least of all the seeds, but when it is grown becomes a great tree for the birds to nest on
B. Just like the seed is small, only a few shall enter into the kingdom of heaven
C. It is easy to overlook
D. It can be ignored but not destroyed

128. What does the parable of the leaven teach about the kingdom of heaven? (Matthew 13:33)

A. The kingdom of heaven continues to expand
B. The kingdom of heaven is very big
C. The Kingdom of God is powerful and has influence! Even though only a little yeast was put on the flour, it was able to get through to every part of the dough
D. The kingdom of heaven is real

129. Who sows the good seed in the world? (Matthew 13:37)

A. The world
B. The Son of Man
C. The sons of the wicked one
D. The angels

WEEK 7 MEMORY VERSE: MATTHEW 18:20

For where two or three are gathered together in My name, I am there in the midst of them.

WEEK 7

130. **What does the "field" represent?** (Matthew 13:38)

A. The world
B. Heaven
C. The church
D. The heart

131. **What is "the good seed"?** (Matthew 13:38)

A. The Word of God
B. The Son of Man
C. The sons of the kingdom
D. The gospel

132. **What are "Tares"?** (Matthew 13:38)

A. The sons of the kingdom
B. The Word
C. The sons of the wicked one
D. False prophets

WEEK 7 MEMORY VERSE: MATTHEW 18:20

For where two or three are gathered together in My name, I am there in the midst of them.

WEEK 7

133. Who is the enemy who sowed the tares? (Matthew 13:39)

A. The Pharisees
B. The devil
C. The world
D. The false prophets

134. What does "the harvest" represent? (Matthew 13:39)

A. The sons of the kingdom
B. The end of the age
C. The angels
D. The devil

135. Who are the "reapers" in the parable of the tares? (Matthew 13:39)

A. Angels
B. The apostles
C. The church
D. Pastors

WEEK 7 MEMORY VERSE: MATTHEW 18:20

For where two or three are gathered together in My name, I am there in the midst of them.

WEEK 7

136. **Which of the following is NOT true about the parable of the wheat and tares? (Matthew 13:40–43)**

A. The wicked will be thrown into the fire
B. The tares will be gathered into the barns
C. The righteous will shine like the sun in the kingdom of their Father
D. None of the above are true

137. **Which of the following does NOT illustrate the Kingdom of Heaven? (Matthew 13:44-46)**

A. It is like a hidden treasure
B. It is like a pearl of great price
C. It is like a dragnet that was cast into the sea & gathered some of every kind
D. It is like a tree with good and bad branches

138. **What does the parable of the dragnet teach us? (Matthew 13:47-50)**

A. The angels will separate the wicked from the just at the end of the age
B. It teaches about fishermen and fish
C. It teaches about sowing and reaping
D. None of the above

WEEK 7 MEMORY VERSE: MATTHEW 18:20

For where two or three are gathered together in My name, I am there in the midst of them.

WEEK 7

139.   What did Jesus say about the scribe instructed about the kingdom of heaven? (Matthew 13:52)

A. He should teach others
B. He is like a householder bringing out new and old treasures
C. He must share what he knows
D. None of the above

140.   Why was Jesus unable to perform many miracles in Nazareth? (Matthew 13:53-58)

A. They saw Him only as the carpenter's son
B. A prophet has no honor in his own hometown
C. Their unbelief limited what He could do
D. All the above

141.   Who did Herod think Jesus was? (Matthew 14:2)

A. The King of the Jews
B. The Son of God
C. The Son of Man
D. John the Baptist, raised from the dead

WEEK 7 MEMORY VERSE: MATTHEW 18:20

For where two or three are gathered together in My name, I am there in the midst of them.

WEEK 7

142. Why did Herod put John the Baptist in jail? (Matthew 14:3-4)

A. Because John rebuked him for marrying Herodias, his brother Philip's wife
B. To please Herodias, who held a grudge against John
C. Because John was gaining popularity
D. Both A and B

143. Why didn't Herod kill John the Baptist right away? (Matthew 14:5)

A. He feared the people, who considered John a prophet
B. He thought John was Jesus's friend
C. John had done no wrong
D. He didn't want to upset Herodias

144. What led Herod to have John the Baptist killed?
(Matthew 14:6-8)

A. Herod feared John's popularity
B. Herodias' daughter asked for John's head after her mother's urging
C. Herod wanted to silence John
D. All the above

WEEK 7 MEMORY VERSE: MATTHEW 18:20

For where two or three are gathered together in My name, I am there in the midst of them.

WEEK 7

145.   What food did the disciples have to feed the 5,000?
(Matthew 14:17)

A. 2 loaves and 5 fish
B. 2 fish and 5 loaves
C. 12 full baskets of fish
D. 12 full baskets of bread

146.   How much food remained after Jesus fed the 5,000?
(Matthew 14:20)

A. 12 baskets of fish
B. 12 baskets of bread
C. 12 baskets of leftovers
D. 7 baskets of leftovers

147.   What happened during the fourth watch of the night?
(Matthew 14:25-33)

A. The disciples thought they saw a ghost walking on water
B. Peter walked on water but began to sink when he doubted
C. The disciples worshiped Jesus, saying, "Truly You are the Son of God"
D. All the above

WEEK 7 MEMORY VERSE: MATTHEW 18:20

For where two or three are gathered together in My name, I am there
in the midst of them.

> "This is the Lord's doing; it is marvelous in my eyes (Psalm 118:23)"

Great job completing the week!

Did you memorize the daily verse?
Test yourself by writing it here...

_____

_____

_____

_____

_____

Use this space to draw a scene from the Bible or reflect on something you learned, felt or experienced...

WEEK 8

148. How were the sick healed at Gennesaret? (Matthew 14:34-36)

A. Jesus touched them, and they were healed
B. Jesus cast out every sickness
C. They begged to touch the hem of His garment, and all who touched Him were healed
D. He laid hands on all the sick

149. How did Jesus respond to accusations about His disciples not washing hands? (Matthew 15:1–11)

A. He called them hypocrites who honored God with their lips but had hearts far from Him
B. He said their traditions had replaced God's commandments
C. He taught that defilement comes from the heart, not from what is eaten
D. All the above

150. What did Jesus say about what defiles a person? (Matthew 15:15–20)

A. What enters the mouth goes to the stomach and is eliminated
B. Evil thoughts and actions that come from the heart defile a person
C. Food is good and doesn't defile
D. Both A and B

WEEK 8 MEMORY VERSE: MATTHEW 19:26

But Jesus looked at them and said to them, "With men this is impossible, but with God all things are possible.

WEEK 8

151.   What caused Jesus to heal the Canaanite woman's daughter? (Matthew 15:21-28)

A. Her tears
B. Her persistent asking
C. Her faith
D. Her humility

152.   What did the Canaanite woman say about dogs eating crumbs? (Matthew 15:26–27)

A. "Even the little dogs eat the crumbs which fall from their master's table"
B. "Please, Lord, I beg You!"
C. She cried and pleaded
D. "You are the Son of David!"

153.   What did Jesus mean by "beware of the leaven of the Pharisees and Sadducees"? (Matthew 16:5–12)

A. Their bread had no faith
B. Their physical food was unclean
C. Their teachings were deceptive and dangerous
D. Their clothes were not holy

WEEK 8 MEMORY VERSE: MATTHEW 19:26

But Jesus looked at them and said to them, "With men this is impossible, but with God all things are possible.

WEEK 8

154. Who revealed to Peter that Jesus was the Christ? (Matthew 16:17)

A. John the Baptist
B. An angel
C. Jesus Himself
D. God the Father

155. What does the name Peter mean? (Matthew 16:18)

A. Rock
B. Redeemed
C. Righteous
D. Ruler

156. Why did Jesus rebuke Peter? (Matthew 16:21-23)

A. Peter was more focused on human things than God's plan
B. Peter didn't understand the suffering Jesus had to endure
C. Jesus discerned that Satan was influencing Peter
D. All the above

WEEK 8 MEMORY VERSE: MATTHEW 19:26
But Jesus looked at them and said to them, "With men this is impossible, but with God all things are possible.

WEEK 8

157. What happened during the transfiguration? (Matthew 17:2–6)

A. Jesus' face shone like the sun, and His clothes became white as light
B. Moses and Elijah appeared
C. A voice from heaven declared Jesus as God's beloved Son
D. All the above

158. Who was Jesus referring to when He said Elijah had already come? (Matthew 17:11–13)

A. Jesus
B. John the Baptist
C. Elisha
D. None of the above

159. Why were the disciples unable to heal the epileptic boy? (Matthew 17:15-21)

A. Their unbelief
B. They needed to fast and pray.
C. None of the above
D. Both A and B

WEEK 8 MEMORY VERSE: MATTHEW 19:26

But Jesus looked at them and said to them, "With men this is impossible, but with God all things are possible.

WEEK 8

160. **How much faith did Jesus say was needed to move a mountain? (Matthew 17:20)**

A. Great faith mixed with action
B. Faith with fasting
C. Faith as small as a mustard seed
D. Faith in yourself

161. **From where did Jesus instruct Peter to get money to pay the temple tax? (Matthew 17:24-27)**

A. From the tax collector
B. From Judas Iscariot, the treasurer
C. In the mouth of the first fish Peter would catch
D. From the temple treasury

162. **Jesus said unless you are converted and become like _____, you will not enter the Kingdom of Heaven. (Matthew 18:3)**

A. Prophets
B. Apostles
C. Little children
D. Spirit-filled leaders

WEEK 8 MEMORY VERSE: MATTHEW 19:26
But Jesus looked at them and said to them, "With men this is impossible, but with God all things are possible.

WEEK 8

163. Who did Jesus say is the greatest in the Kingdom of Heaven? (Matthew 18:4)

A. Children
B. Those who act like children
C. Anyone who humbles themselves like a child
D. Those full of spiritual gifts

164. Receiving a little child in Jesus' name is like receiving who? (Matthew 18:5)

A. A prophet
B. Jesus Himself
C. The Holy Spirit
D. God the Father

165. What did Jesus say would be better for someone who causes a child to sin? (Matthew 18:6)

A. A millstone was hung around his neck, and he was drowned in the sea
B. To be cast into the fire
C. To cut off the thing that caused the sin
D. To seek forgiveness from a prophet

WEEK 8 MEMORY VERSE: MATTHEW 19:26
But Jesus looked at them and said to them, "With men this is impossible, but with God all things are possible.

WEEK 8

166. What should you do if your hand or eye causes you to sin? (Matthew 18:8-9)

A. Ask God for forgiveness
B. Pray about it
C. Cut it off or pluck it out and cast it from you
D. Wait for deliverance

167. What did Jesus teach through the parable of the lost sheep? (Matthew 18:12-14)

A. Everyone is valuable to God
B. God does not want anyone to perish — each person is valuable
C. Both A and B
D. None of the above

168. How should you respond if a brother sins against you? (Matthew 18:15-17)

A. Go alone and tell him his fault. If he doesn't hear you, take one or two witnesses, if he doesn't hear them, tell the Church
B. Ignore them
C. Ask someone to go with you and tell him his fault
D. Pray for him

WEEK 8 MEMORY VERSE: MATTHEW 19:26

But Jesus looked at them and said to them, "With men this is impossible, but with God all things are possible.

"

For my shame and trouble, I receive a double portion from the Lord

(Isaiah 61:7)

"

Great job completing the week!

Did you memorize the daily verse?
Test yourself by writing it here...

_____

_____

_____

_____

_____

Use this space to draw a scene from the Bible or reflect on something you learned, felt or experienced...

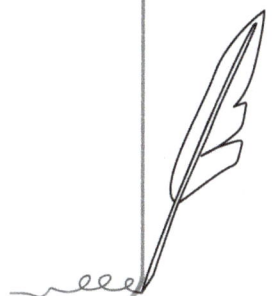

169.   How often did Jesus say we should forgive? (Matthew 18:22)

A. Up to seven times
B. Up to seventy times seven (all the time)
C. Up to seventy-seven times
D. Up to seven hundred times

**170.   What was the lesson in the parable of the unforgiving servant?
(Matthew 18:23–35)**

A. God is a merciful and forgiving God
B. God expects us to show mercy as He has shown us mercy
C. God will not forgive us if we are unwilling to forgive others
D. All the above

171.   What did Jesus teach about divorce? (Matthew 19:3-9)

A. A man shall leave his parents and be joined to his wife
B. Moses allowed divorce due to hardened hearts
C. Divorce outside of sexual immorality leads to adultery
D. All the above

WEEK 9 MEMORY VERSE: MATTHEW 21:22
If you believe, you will receive whatever you ask for in prayer.

WEEK 9

172. What did Jesus teach about celibacy? (Matthew 19:11-12)

A. Some are born eunuchs
B. Some are made eunuchs by others
C. Some choose celibacy for the Kingdom of Heaven
D. All the above

173. What did Jesus tell the rich young ruler to do to have eternal life? (Matthew 19:16–21)

A. Sell everything
B. Follow Jesus
C. Give to the poor
D. Sell all, give to the poor, then follow Him

174. What did Jesus say was easier than a rich man entering the Kingdom? (Matthew 19:23–24)

A. Being born again
B. A camel going through the eye of a needle
C. Finding God
D. Finding a pearl of great price

WEEK 9 MEMORY VERSE: MATTHEW 21:22
If you believe, you will receive whatever you ask for in prayer.

WEEK 9

175. What reward is given to those who leave everything to follow Jesus? (Matthew 19:27–30)

A. They will sit on thrones judging Israel
B. They will receive a hundredfold and eternal life
C. They will be known as Jesus' chosen ones
D. Both A and B

176. What was Jesus' message in the parable of the workers of the vineyard? (Matthew 20:1–16)

A. The last will be first, and the first last
B. God is just in rewarding as He chooses
C. Many are called, but few are chosen
D. All the above

177. Who will sit at Jesus' right and left hand in glory? (Matthew 20:20–23)

A. Peter and John
B. James and John
C. It is for those the Father has chosen
D. This was not addressed in Scripture

WEEK 9 MEMORY VERSE: MATTHEW 21:22
If you believe, you will receive whatever you ask for in prayer.

WEEK 9

178. What must someone do to be great or first in God's Kingdom?
(Matthew 20:26–27)

A. Those that desire to be great, let them be servants
B. Those that desire to be first, let them be slaves of all
C. Both A and B
D. None of the above

179. What did Jesus say was the purpose for which He came?
(Matthew 20:28)

A. To set captives free
B. To serve and to give His life a ransom for many
C. To reign on the throne of David
D. To teach and perform miracles

180. When Jesus neared Jerusalem, what animal did He send for?
(Matthew 21:2)

A. A camel
B. A donkey
C. A lion
D. A calf

WEEK 9 MEMORY VERSE: MATTHEW 21:22
If you believe, you will receive whatever you ask for in prayer.

WEEK 9

181. **Why did Jesus drive out those who were buying and selling in the temple? (Matthew 21:12–13)**
A. "It is written, 'My house shall be called a house of prayer,' but you have made it a den of thieves"
B. "It is written, 'Remember the Sabbath day, to keep it holy'"
C. "It is written, 'I am the Lord your God; you shall have no other gods before Me'"
D. "It is written, 'The Sabbath is holy unto the Lord'"

182. **What was Jesus' response concerning how the fig tree withered away so soon? (Matthew 21:20-22)**

A. If you have faith and don't doubt, you can do things like this and more
B. If you have faith, you can command a mountain to be cast into the sea, and it will happen
C. If you believe, you will receive whatever you ask for in prayer
D. All the above

183. **What lesson did Jesus teach with the parable of the two sons? (Matthew 21:28–32)**
A. Sinners would enter the Kingdom before the religious leaders
B. John the Baptist showed the way of righteousness, but the leaders did not believe him
C. Even when they saw sinners repent, the leaders still refused to believe and change
D. All the above

WEEK 9 MEMORY VERSE: MATTHEW 21:22
If you believe, you will receive whatever you ask for in prayer.

WEEK 9

184. Which scripture did Jesus say was fulfilled by the parable of the wicked vinedressers? (Matthew 21:33-42)

A. The stone which the builders rejected has become the chief cornerstone
B. For I was hungry, and you didn't feed me
C. Give, and it will be given to you
D. I am the vine; you are the branches

185. What was Jesus' key message in the parable of the wedding feast? (Matthew 22:1–14)

A. Go and make disciples of all
B. Many are called, but few are chosen
C. Come and let us reason together
D. You are the salt and the light of this world

186. How did Jesus respond when the Pharisees tried to trap Him with a question about paying taxes to Caesar? (Matthew 22:15–21)

A. He remained silent and avoided their question
B. He asked for a coin and said, "Render to Caesar what is Caesar's, and to God what is God's"
C. He condemned their wickedness and warned of judgment
D. He reminded them to be wise as serpents and gentle as doves

WEEK 9 MEMORY VERSE: MATTHEW 21:22
If you believe, you will receive whatever you ask for in prayer.

187. When asked about the greatest commandment, how did Jesus summarize the entire Law? (Matthew 22:34–40)

A. "Love the Lord your God with all your heart, soul, and mind"
B. "Love your neighbor as yourself"
C. "Remember the Sabbath and keep it holy"
D. A and B together

188. What question did Jesus ask to reveal the true identity of the Messiah? (Matthew 22:41–45)

A. "How does David, inspired by the Spirit, call Him 'Lord'?"
B. "If David calls Him 'Lord,' how then is He his Son?"
C. "Is Joseph really My father?"
D. Both A and B

189. Which Prophet spoke about the abomination of desolation? (Matthew 24:15)

A. Isaiah
B. Jeremiah
C. Micah
D. Daniel

WEEK 9 MEMORY VERSE: MATTHEW 21:22
If you believe, you will receive whatever you ask for in prayer.

"

I am my Father's child. I am always with Him and all that He has is mine (Luke 15:31)

"

Great job completing the week!

Did you memorize the daily verse?
Test yourself by writing it here...

_____

_____

_____

_____

_____

Use this space to draw a scene from the Bible or reflect on something you learned, felt or experienced...

WEEK 10

190. Why did Jesus say the days of tribulation would be shortened? (Matthew 24:22)

A. For the sake of the elect, that they might be saved
B. So that people would repent before it's too late
C. Because God decided to change His mind
D. So that Satan's plans could be fully stopped

191. What cosmic signs did Jesus say would follow the great tribulation? (Matthew 24:29)

A. The sun will go dark, the moon will not shine, stars will fall, and the heavens will shake
B. The heavens will light up with glory and fire
C. The sky will open and angels will descend
D. The stars will fall and worship the Son of Man

192. Jesus said, "Heaven and earth will pass away, but ___ will never pass away." (Matthew 24:35)

A. The glory of God the Father
B. The words of Jesus
C. The kingdom of heaven
D. The miraculous signs of Jesus

WEEK 10 MEMORY VERSE: MATTHEW 22:37
Jesus said to him, 'You shall love the Lord your God with all your heart, with all your soul, and with all your mind.'

WEEK 10

193. Who alone knows the exact day and hour of Jesus' return?
(Matthew 24:36)

A. Only the Father
B. The Father and the Holy Spirit
C. The angels in heaven
D. The prophets

194. Why did Jesus urge His followers to stay alert and watchful?
(Matthew 24:42–44)

A. He will come like a thief at a time that no one knows
B. He will come at an hour we do not expect
C. Both A and B
D. None of the above

195. Who does Jesus say is the faithful and wise servant?
(Matthew 24:45-50)

A. The one that can be trusted with managing the master's household and the other servants
B. The one who does not beat his fellow servants or eat and drink with the drunkards
C. The one who will be found faithful at the unexpected return of the master
D. All the above

WEEK 10 MEMORY VERSE: MATTHEW 22:37
Jesus said to him, 'You shall love the Lord your God with all your heart, with all your soul, and with all your mind.'

196. **What powerful truth does Jesus teach in the parable of the ten virgins? (Matthew 25:1–13)**

A. The dangers of pride
B. We need to be humble
C. The unexpected return of the Son of Man
D. The importance of remaining a virgin until marriage

197. **What is the main message in the parable of talents? (Matthew 25:29)**

A. Those who steward their gifts faithfully will be entrusted with more
B. Giving to others is the secret to increase
C. If you do nothing with your gifts, even what you have will be taken
D. Both A and C

198. **What will Jesus say to the righteous 'sheep' on His right hand? (Matthew 25:31–34)**

A. "Enter the kingdom, for when you loved others, you loved Me"
B. "You served well and will be rewarded"
C. "Welcome, good and faithful servant"
D. "Because you clothed, fed, and visited Me, enter My joy"

WEEK 10 MEMORY VERSE: MATTHEW 22:37

Jesus said to him, 'You shall love the Lord your God with all your heart, with all your soul, and with all your mind.'

WEEK 10

199. What will Jesus say to the 'goats' on His left hand? (Matthew 25:41–46)

A. "Depart from Me into everlasting fire, for you rejected Me when you ignored the least of these"
B. "You had your chance and missed it"
C. "You were careless with grace"
D. "You chose your own way instead of Mine"

200. After what feast did Jesus declare that He would be handed over to be crucified? (Matthew 26:1–2)

A. The Feast of Tabernacles
B. The Pentecost
C. The Passover
D. Good Friday

201. Why did Jesus praise the woman who poured costly oil on His head from an alabaster flask? (Matthew 26:6–12)

A. Because she chose expensive oil
B. Because she was joyful in serving
C. Because she anointed Him in preparation for His burial
D. Because she was His close friend

WEEK 10 MEMORY VERSE: MATTHEW 22:37
Jesus said to him, 'You shall love the Lord your God with all your heart, with all your soul, and with all your mind.'

WEEK 10

202. **Which of Jesus' disciples agreed to betray Him for money? (Matthew 26:14-15)**

A. James
B. Peter
C. Judas Iscariot
D. John

203. **How did Jesus reveal the identity of the one who would betray Him? (Matthew 26:20–24)**

A. He who sat closest to Him
B. He who dipped his hand in the bowl with Him
C. He who would kiss Him on the cheek
D. He who would bow before Him

204. **What did Jesus say is the purpose of eating His body and drinking His blood? (Matthew 26:26-28)**

A. It was a sign of the new covenant to forgive the sins of many
B. It was a reminder to always eat and drink together
C. It was a reminder of the importance of fellowship
D. None of the above

WEEK 10 MEMORY VERSE: MATTHEW 22:37
Jesus said to him, 'You shall love the Lord your God with all your heart, with all your soul, and with all your mind.'

WEEK 10

205.   Which disciple did Jesus say would deny Him three times before the rooster crowed? (Matthew 26:33–35)

A. Peter
B. John
C. Judas
D. James

206.   What was the name of the garden where Jesus prayed before His arrest? (Matthew 26:36)

A. Gethsemane
B. Mount Sinai
C. Golgotha
D. Eden

207.   What did Jesus pray in deep anguish before His arrest? (Matthew 26:39–44)

A. "Father, let this cup pass from Me"
B. "Nevertheless, not My will, but Yours be done"
C. "If this cup cannot pass unless I drink it, Your will be done"
D. All of the above

WEEK 10 MEMORY VERSE: MATTHEW 22:37
Jesus said to him, 'You shall love the Lord your God with all your heart, with all your soul, and with all your mind.'

WEEK 10

208. What signal did Judas use to betray Jesus to the authorities? (Matthew 26:48–49)

A. A handshake
B. A kiss
C. A whispered name
D. A respectful bow

209. What sin, punishable by death, was Jesus falsely accused of? (Matthew 26:57-66)

A. Deceiving the people
B. Breaking Sabbath law
C. Blasphemy
D. Threatening to destroy the temple

210. Why did Peter cry bitterly after the rooster crowed? (Matthew 26:69-75)

A. Because he witnessed Jesus' suffering
B. Because he lost sight of the other disciples
C. Because he denied Jesus three times, just as Jesus had foretold
D. Because he felt powerless to help Jesus

WEEK 10 MEMORY VERSE: MATTHEW 22:37
Jesus said to him, 'You shall love the Lord your God with all your heart, with all your soul, and with all your mind.'

"
The Lord has given me wisdom, knowledge, and understanding (Proverbs 2:6)
"

Great job completing the week!

Did you memorize the daily verse?
Test yourself by writing it here...

_____

_____

_____

_____

_____

_____

Use this space to draw a scene from the Bible or reflect on something you learned, felt or experienced...

WEEK 11

211. What was the name of the Roman governor the religious leaders brought Jesus to? (Matthew 27:1–2)

A. Caiaphas
B. Barabbas
C. Pontius Pilate
D. Herod

212. What did Judas Iscariot do after realizing the weight of his betrayal? (Matthew 27:3–5)

A. He confessed he had sinned
B. He returned the silver
C. He took his own life
D. All the above

213. How did Judas Iscariot die? (Matthew 27:5)

A. He hanged himself
B. He killed himself with the sword
C. He threw himself into the river
D. He threw himself into a fire

WEEK 11 MEMORY VERSE: MATTHEW 28:19
Go therefore and make disciples of all the nations, baptizing them in the name of the Father and of the Son and of the Holy Spirit.

WEEK 11

214. Which prisoner did the multitude demand be released instead of Jesus Christ? (Matthew 27:15-21)

A. Barabbas
B. Beelzebub
C. Barnabas
D. Bartholomew

215. Why did Pontius Pilate hesitate to crucify Jesus? (Matthew 27:17–24)

A. He knew it was out of envy the leaders accused Jesus
B. His wife warned him in a dream
C. He found no fault in Jesus
D. All the above

216. What symbolic act did Pilate perform to show he did not want to be held responsible for Jesus' death? (Matthew 27:24)

A. He washed his face with water
B. He washed his hands before the crowd
C. He sprinkled water on the ground
D. He lay before Jesus in silence

WEEK 11 MEMORY VERSE: MATTHEW 28:19
Go therefore and make disciples of all the nations, baptizing them in the name of the Father and of the Son and of the Holy Spirit.

WEEK 11

217. Who helped Jesus carry the cross to where He was crucified?
(Matthew 27:32)

A. Peter
B. John
C. Simon of Cyrene
D. Matthew

218. What is the name of the place where Jesus was crucified?
(Matthew 27:33)

A. Gethsemane
B. Golgotha
C. Jerusalem
D. Calvary

219. What does "Golgotha" mean? (Matthew 27:33)

A. A place of torment
B. A place of a skull
C. A place of bones
D. A place of sorrow

WEEK 11 MEMORY VERSE: MATTHEW 28:19
Go therefore and make disciples of all the nations, baptizing them in
the name of the Father and of the Son and of the Holy Spirit.

WEEK 11

220. What did the soldiers give Jesus to drink at Golgotha? (Matthew 27:34)

A. Wine mixed with gall
B. Fresh water
C. Vinegar
D. Grape juice

221. What was the accusation written against Jesus and placed on His cross? (Matthew 27:37)

A. This is Jesus the King of the Jews
B. This is Jesus, the blasphemer
C. This is Jesus, the murderer
D. This is Jesus, the accuser

222. Who was crucified alongside Jesus? (Matthew 27:38)

A. Two robbers, one on His right and the other on His left
B. Two murderers, one on His right and the other on His left
C. A murderer and a thief
D. One thief and one soldier

WEEK 11 MEMORY VERSE: MATTHEW 28:19
Go therefore and make disciples of all the nations, baptizing them in the name of the Father and of the Son and of the Holy Spirit.

WEEK 11

223. How did the crowd mock Jesus as He hung on the cross?
(Matthew 27:39–43)

A. They told Him to save Himself if He was the Son of God
B. They told Him to come down if He was truly the King of Israel
C. They said God should rescue Him if He delighted in Him
D. All the above

224. What happened from the sixth hour to the ninth hour as Jesus hung on the cross? (Matthew 27:45)

A. There was weeping throughout Jerusalem
B. The earth trembled with thunder
C. Darkness covered the land
D. A bright light shone upon the hill

225. At what hour did Jesus give up His Spirit, and what did He say?
(Matthew 27:46)

A. At the ninth hour. He said "Eli, Eli, lama sabachthani?"
B. At the ninth hour. He said "My God, My God, why have you forsaken me?"
C. Both A and B
D. None of the above

WEEK 11 MEMORY VERSE: MATTHEW 28:19

Go therefore and make disciples of all the nations, baptizing them in the name of the Father and of the Son and of the Holy Spirit.

WEEK 11

226. What miraculous events occurred when Jesus gave up His Spirit? (Matthew 27:50–53)

A. The temple veil was torn in two
B. The earth shook and rocks split open
C. Graves were opened and saints were raised to life
D. All the above

227. Who was the rich man who asked for Jesus' body and buried Him in a new tomb? (Matthew 27:57)

A. Joseph of Arimathea
B. Joseph of Galilee
C. Joseph the Nazarene
D. Joseph of Cupertino

228. Why did the religious leaders ask Pilate to place guards at Jesus' tomb? (Matthew 27:62–64)

A. They were afraid the disciples would steal His body and claim He had risen
B. They wanted to show respect for the dead
C. They believed Jesus might still be alive
D. They wanted to keep people away from the tomb

WEEK 11 MEMORY VERSE: MATTHEW 28:19
Go therefore and make disciples of all the nations, baptizing them in the name of the Father and of the Son and of the Holy Spirit.

WEEK 11

229. What did the chief priests do when the guards reported that Jesus had risen? (Matthew 28:11–15)

A. They knelt down in repentance
B. They dismissed the guards as liars
C. They bribed the guards to spread a false story
D. They punished the guards and blamed the disciples

230. In what City did Jesus first appear to His disciples? (Matthew 28:16)

A. Jerusalem
B. Galilee
C. Bethlehem
D. Nazareth

231. What final command did Jesus give to His disciples before ascending? (Matthew 28:18–20)

A. To go into all the world to make disciples
B. To make disciples and baptize them in the name of the Father, the Son, and the Holy Spirit
C. To teach the disciples to observe all things that Jesus had taught them
D. All the above

WEEK 11 MEMORY VERSE: MATTHEW 28:19
Go therefore and make disciples of all the nations, baptizing them in the name of the Father and of the Son and of the Holy Spirit.

"

The Lord increases my greatness and comforts me on every side (Psalm 71:21)

"

Great job completing the week!

Did you memorize the daily verse?
Test yourself by writing it here...

_____

_____

_____

_____

_____

_____

Use this space to draw a scene from the Bible or reflect
on something you learned, felt or experienced...

Certificate of Completion

This Certificate Certifies That:

_____

Has Successfully Completed The Matthew Workbook!

Flo & Grace

_____

PARENT/TEACHER SIGNATURE

PROJECT KINGDOM COME

WOULD YOU LIKE TO ACCEPT JESUS INTO YOUR HEART?

THE BIBLE SAYS:

If you confess with your mouth that Jesus is Lord and believe in your heart that God has raised Him from the dead, you will be saved
(Romans 10:9)

SAY THE PRAYER BELOW OUT LOUD AND BELIEVE IT IN YOUR HEART!

Dear Lord Jesus,
I know that I am a sinner, and I ask for Your forgiveness.
I believe You died for my sins and rose from the dead.
I repent of my sins and invite You to come into my heart and life.
I want to trust and follow You as my Lord and Savior. Help me to live for you for the rest of my life.
I am now a child of God, and I ask You to fill me with Your Holy Spirit.

In Jesus' Name I pray, Amen.

Congratulations!
If you have prayed this prayer, please let an adult know or send an email to mybibleworkbooks@gmail.com

ANSWER KEY:

1. C	13. D	25. D	37. B
2. C	14. A	26. C	38. B
3. D	15. B	27. B	39. D
4. D	16. D	28. B	40. D
5. A	17. D	29. D	41. A
6. B	18. C	30. C	42. D
7. A	19. A	31. A	43. D
8. D	20. B	32. A	44. D
9. C	21. B	33. B	45. D
10. B	22. B	34. C	46. D
11. B	23. A	35. D	47. D
12. C	24. C	36. C	48. D

ANSWER KEY:

49. D	61. A	73. A	85. A
50. B	62. D	74. D	86. D
51. A	63. A	75. D	87. C
52. D	64. C	76. D	88. A
53. D	65. A	77. A	89. C
54. D	66. A	78. D	90. A
55. C	67. C	79. D	91. D
56. D	68. D	80. B	92. A
57. A	69. D	81. A	93. D
58. A	70. A	82. D	94. A
59. A	71. C	83. C	95. C
60. D	72. C	84. D	96. D

97. B	109. C	121. D	133. B
98. D	110. C	122. A	134. B
99. A	111. A	123. B	135. A
100. B	112. D	124. D	136. B
101. D	113. C	125. C	137. D
102. B	114. C	126. D	138. A
103. A	115. D	127. A	139. B
104. C	116. B	128. C	140. D
105. A	117. B	129. B	141. D
106. A	118. D	130. A	142. A
107. D	119. A	131. C	143. A
108. C	120. C	132. C	144. B

 **ANSWER KEY:**

145. B	157. D	169. B	181. A
146. C	158. B	170. D	182. D
147. D	159. D	171. D	183. D
148. C	160. C	172. D	184. A
149. D	161. C	173. D	185. B
150. D	162. C	174. B	186. B
151. C	163. C	175. D	187. D
152. A	164. B	176. D	188. D
153. C	165. A	177. C	189. D
154. D	166. C	178. C	190. A
155. A	167. C	179. B	191. A
156. D	168. A	180. B	192. B

ANSWER KEY:

193. A	205. A	217. C	
194. C	206. A	218. B	
195. D	207. D	219. B	
196. C	208. B	220. A	
197. D	209. C	221. A	229. C
198. D	210. C	222. A	230. B
199. A	211. C	223. D	231. D
200. C	212. D	224. C	
201. C	213. A	225. C	
202. C	214. A	226. D	
203. B	215. D	227. A	
204. A	216. B	228. A	

PLEASE GIVE US YOUR FEEDBACK!

Please send us your feedback on this workbook. We would love to hear what you enjoyed most, and ways you think it could be improved!

Please Send an email to: MyBibleWorkbooks@gmail.com, or leave us a comment on one of our social media pages.

MyBibleWorkbooks@gmail.com

Projectkingdomcome

Projectkingdomcome

SCAN ME

> And I am certain that God, who began the good work within you, will continue His work until it is finally finished on the day when Christ Jesus returns.
> Philippians 1:6

DRAW HERE

DRAW HERE

DRAW HERE

DRAW HERE

DRAW HERE